Is There An Elephant In The Room?

Loving Your Spouse Through Chronic Illness

D1715727

By: Donna Sue Peros, RN, BSN, M.S.

CONTENTS

Introduction

It is my sincere hope that this book will impress upon the reader the profound impact of faith in God in securing one's life during the most traumatic times. Prayer has always been a major means of communication with God throughout my life, and he has never failed me. Life often takes cruel and unexpected turns, but it is only through God that we can find the peace that surpasses all understanding in such moments.

I am immensely grateful for my Christian upbringing, as it has given me the strength to endure the storms of life.

Through sharing our story, my ultimate aspiration is to offer assistance to those who are grappling with the many challenges presented by chronic illness as they seek solace in God to navigate their battles.

Dedication

I dedicate this book to my husband, who has been a brave and strong example of living the Christian faith in the face of chronic illness. His unwavering commitment to his beliefs has been a source of inspiration for me. I also dedicate this book to my 39-year-old nephew, J. D. Turley, who tragically passed away from Glioblastoma while I was in the process of writing. Both of these remarkable men had a deep desire to lead others to Christ, and their testimonies influenced countless souls to seek Jesus.

If you find yourself in the midst of the chaos caused by chronic illness, it is important to remember that many people have successfully managed their conditions and continue to lead fulfilling lives. Not all chronic illnesses lead to fatal outcomes.

Regardless of your circumstances, I hope this book will provide valuable insights on how to communicate effectively with your healthcare providers and your family, as these connections can significantly impact your relationships and overall well-being."

I would like to express my appreciation to my editor, Celeste Ava, for the assistance and encouragement in this journey.

What can I say regarding the endless support and skill my son-in-law, Paul Helmick, gave me from beginning to end? Thank you.

Chapter 1

The Fast Track

Many events that occur early in a person's life have a profound impact on their emotional and spiritual development. My own experiences were no exception, except for one sincere decision I made at the age of 6 - to be a Christian. That decision has never changed; it has remained steadfast throughout my life. In my story, I will reveal the intimate ways in which God has guided and protected me amidst life's numerous trials.

My life was set on the fast track from a very early age. Social expectations meant for much older children were placed upon me when I was very young. In elementary school, it was a common practice to 'double promote' children who were academically achieving above the standard for their age or grade. Unfortunately, little attention or assessment was given to the developmental appropriateness or social development of the child in question. It was not a cruel attempt to be abusive to the high-achieving student. At that time, research studies emphasizing social development and the long-term effects of these academic decisions had not been completed yet. Academic achievement was considered the single most important deciding factor.

In the small rural schools of the 1960s, each classroom had 25 to 30 students, making it practically impossible to group students according to their abilities within the appropriate age level.

Consequently, everyone was taught at the same pace and on the same material. The limited number of teachers in the school resulted in grouping students by placing them in a higher grade if they showed a need to progress further in the curriculum. As a result, I was 'double promoted' from third to fourth grade.

All of the conditions mentioned above, combined with the fact that I had a September birthday, meant that I was extremely unprepared developmentally, physically, and socially for the years ahead. This single decision during such crucial formative years profoundly impacted my self-image and confidence and triggered a rollercoaster of emotions throughout my remaining school years. Did I fail? No, quite the opposite; overachieving became my predominant motivating force. Early on, I learned to rely on God during difficult times. Thanks to the strong faith of my parents, I was introduced to salvation and learned how to depend on God on a daily basis. As my faith matured, so did my ability to cope with life and its challenges.

Due to the constant fear of not succeeding and the looming threat of 'not being promoted,' which was reinforced by my parents, I became an anxious and fearful individual. I struggled to achieve the highest grades, always striving for an 'A.' The pressure placed by teachers and my parents at such a young age, with statements like 'you were double promoted, but if you don't complete this work satisfactorily or read this many books by this date, you will be held back next year,' eventually became self-imposed as time went on.

After completing the 8th grade in my small community school, I moved on to 9th grade since there were no middle schools or junior high schools in my rural district at that time. I faced a competitive school environment as students from various feeder schools came together. It was quite challenging, especially considering I was only 13 years old when I entered high school. Puberty hadn't even begun to affect my confused existence at that point. Once on the fast-track train, there seemed to be no way to get off.

There were very limited social activities to provide a means to mature appropriately. If you wanted to participate in sports, your parents had to drive you to and from practice, as the school was located 35 minutes away from home on winding, narrow mountain roads. Both my parents had demanding work schedules: my mother worked the day shift and took night college classes, while my father worked the midnight shift an hour away from home. My mother was a teacher at the local elementary school and took night classes to maintain her required certification, while my father worked as an electrician in the coal mines, consistently on the midnight or evening shift throughout my life. Unfortunately, I had no means of transportation for school activities, and there were very few activities offered by our local church.

Some of the communities where my peers lived had a higher economic status and were more urban. They had theaters and a variety of community activities, allowing them to form close bonds. These students seemed more confident, dressed impeccably in outfits that matched the latest fashion trends, and appeared less stressed about their academic achievements. The girls had fashionable hairstyles and looked much more attractive than I felt, while the guys were remarkably handsome. I had new clothes, but they wore the latest fashion and makeup! It wasn't long before I overheard discussions about academic competition and class rank, with that process starting as early as 9th grade.

All that being said, amidst those struggling years, I developed and matured in another area. I became highly dependent on my spiritual network, primarily consisting of adult mentors, and my belief in God became a central part of my existence. Coming from a very strict spiritual background and church, I refrained from participating in normal social events, as they were deemed sinful or wrong in my mind for many years. In fact, it wasn't until after my second year of college and graduation from nursing school that I started to reconsider these beliefs. I never wore pants, except for gym, where uniforms were required. I kept my hair uncut, with its length reaching below my waist. I abstained from watching TV, going to movies, or attending dances, as these were considered 'men's traditions' and were seen as complete 'No-No's' by the church I attended and the adults who guided my faith.

Although my views on salvation and Christian living have matured with God's help over the years, I now recognize a purpose that God may have had for me during those formative years. As a young girl trying to please, I followed the legalistic instructions set by others, even though they may appear overly strict in hindsight, believing it to be the Christian way. I respect that such rules are essential for some believers, and I will never criticize another person's beliefs or convictions. It's important to note that I actually graduated from high school at the age of 16 and entered college a few weeks before turning 17. I vividly remember the challenge imprinted in my mind during that first semester when I had an atheist professor for English 101 and 102 who singled me out in front of the class. He asked me to write three words on the board that came to mind when I thought of the word 'Spring.' One of my phrases included 'God.' He instructed me to erase 'God.' While I don't recall the exact discussion that followed in front of the class, I felt a sense of accomplishment for expressing my beliefs at the beginning. I felt God's strength at that moment. Surprisingly, the professor gave me A's in his classes and never challenged me again. That experience contributed to my spiritual growth and maturity.

By the age of 19, I had graduated from nursing school and began caring for patients at the hospital, encountering life-and-death situations on a daily basis. If I had been distracted by the typical social events of a teenager during those years, I genuinely believe my life would have taken a different path. I believe there was a purpose in the way my spiritual growth and maturity unfolded and how God guided my life. Was I ever self-righteous or judgmental towards others? No, deep down in my heart, I never felt that my friends needed to follow the same path I was on. However, due to my strict behaviors, there were many lonely days during that time in my life when my friends believed I held different opinions. That truly saddened my young heart. Often, I wasn't included in everyday discussions at school because I wasn't part of the social network.

Nevertheless, many of the kids treated me like one of their own, and one best friend was intrigued by my nature and welcomed me into her home countless times over the years. Many other friends were kind and treated me well. Eventually, I found an outlet through the Bible

Club, Student Council, Patriotic Committee, and other organizations that prepared me for college. I made lifelong friends and found my place. I devoted my full time to academics, participated in special science fairs, and studied diligently. God rewarded me by making me one of the two valedictorians of my class.

Skip forward to college. God had definitely called me to become a registered nurse, and despite my young age, I successfully completed the program in just 2 1/2 years after high school. I began working immediately after passing my board exams at the age of 19.

I witnessed the hand of God guiding me over the next several years. After working different nursing positions for seven years and encountering various experiences, I found myself still living at home with my parents. I commuted 45 minutes to work in Charleston, WV. However, as a single female, my income did not allow me to afford rent and to move out on my own. Despite holding a nursing degree, my monthly earnings were approximately $600, even while working full-time on the night shift. Although it was considered decent pay, it wasn't enough to cover expenses such as car payments, rent, and utilities.

Around this time, my mother decided to transfer to a different school within our county after having worked at the same school for a long time. One day, she came home and began discussing the son of a colleague she had been working with. He had served in the Air Force for four years and was about to be honorably discharged. As I pieced the story together, I realized that it was Bert Ricky Peros, whom I had known as Bert back in high school. What were the odds of such a peculiar occurrence happening? I only knew Rick's cousin, Sharon, so the chances of us reconnecting after high school seemed unlikely unless my mother had changed jobs that year. However, we didn't immediately get in touch. I kept urging my mother to ask more questions: When would he be returning home? When was his Air Force service ending? Could she inquire with Pauline, his mother, to have him contact me?

Now, anyone who knew my mother would understand that she was a very proper lady at work. It took a lot of persuasion on my part, but she finally gathered the courage to break her decorum and inquire about Pauline's eldest son. And guess what? Some members of Rick's family recalled me as that devout Christian girl from one of the stricter churches in our community, and they were hesitant to "connect" the two of us. I later discovered that some of the family had different girls in mind for Rick, but what they had forgotten was that he was a fiercely independent individual. Thankfully, Sharon, his cousin who had grown up with him like a sister, came to my defense and encouraged him to give me a call. If it hadn't been for Cousin Sharon and God's intervention, Rick and I probably wouldn't have had that initial phone conversation when he was on leave. His family had developed a misguided preconception of "what I would be like" based on their past experiences with individuals from churches that shared similar beliefs to mine. Isn't that something we all tend to do? It serves as a valuable lesson for all of us: people often judge all Christians based on their interactions with individual Christians they know. It's crucial that we reflect God's love in our lives. As time went on, Rick's sister grew to love me and became an integral part of our lives.

At that time, I was working the midnight shift as a registered nurse in the newborn nursery in Charleston, WV. Since I hadn't heard from Ricky, Mrs. Peros' son, I decided to go on a date with an engineer whom my colleagues at work had introduced me to. Unfortunately, the experience wasn't a positive one, and after a couple of dates with the handsome engineer from Pennsylvania, I began distancing myself and keeping our phone conversations short. Around the same time, I visited my dear grandmother, Mamaw Turley, when a phone call came in for me. Initially, I thought it was the engineer calling, so I was about to end the conversation when I asked, "who is this?" The person on the other end replied, "who do you think it is?" I was utterly confused until the guy finally revealed himself as Rick Peros! We talked for what seemed like hours that day, reconnecting after seven years.

After several more calls, he decided to ask me out. He was on leave from the Air Force and stationed at the White House in Washington, DC. He could potentially be discharged soon, having completed his four years of service. However, it was a significant decision for him because the Air Force was pressuring him to re-enlist. The cryptographic branch, in which he was trained, required a considerable investment from the Air Force in terms of training and clearance. Out of 2,000 recruits, only two were typically chosen for this highly specialized work that involved secret service clearance. I later learned some details about his role and how he was selected, but he didn't speak much about it due to the confidential nature and security clearance associated with his position. Therefore, after our last phone call and a few dates, he informed me that he had to return for one month to decide whether he would come home or stay in the Air Force.

Now, there is one part that I omitted. From the moment of our first date, I was head over heels in love. I knew from day one that I had met the love of my life. However, the question remained: Was it meant to be? The following four weeks were incredibly stressful for me as I anxiously wondered whether he would choose to stay in the Air Force or come home. During this time, I sincerely prayed for God's will to be done in our lives.

I recently stumbled upon a "nest" of old letters, poems, and cards that I had sent him during those days. He had hidden them away on the back of a closet shelf, upsurging our sweet old memories. As I read through them, tears welled up in my eyes, and I was instantly transported back to those cherished moments we shared.

Then it happened—a sign that things were in motion! I was working the midnight shift in the newborn nursery when the phone rang, and the switchboard operator informed me that I had a call from the White House. What? Rick had thought it would be exciting for me to receive a call from the White House. However, what he didn't realize was that the hospital had a gossip network known as the "rumor mill," and there were no secrets when it came to fellow employees. By the time I went to dinner during that shift, heads turned, and whispers spread. There I was, the girl who received that "White House" call. I'm not sure how far the rumors traveled that night, but I probably ended up being some kind of secret agent in the stories that circulated. It made me feel special that night, and the wonderful thing was that Rick Peros would continue to make me feel truly special in many more ways as time went on.

****

(In the years of my upbringing, I prayed for God to direct and bring an individual into my life that would be pleasing to Him:"Be ye steadfast, unmovable, always abounding in the work of the Lord." I Cor. 15:58 KJV)

Chapter 2

In Love - Our Life Began

The weeks passed by slowly, but when I received the next correspondence from Rick, he informed me that he would definitely be coming home upon his official honorable discharge from the USAF. He had fulfilled his duty with honor but was ready to return home. We started dating, and soon after his arrival, a heartbreaking event unfolded. His beloved Grandma Julia Piros, the person closest to him in the entire world, suddenly fell ill. He took me to Coronary Care to meet her. Grandma Julia was a true legend to Rick, and he had hoped that I could have known her for a longer period of time and learned recipes directly from her, passed down from her native Hungary. She had traveled across the ocean in a small boat with only limited possessions (some of which the family still possesses today). However, instead of the quality time he desired with her, his beloved Grandma passed away as soon as he safely returned from his military service. He was utterly heartbroken, and I had never seen him grieve in such a profound way before. He wept bitterly, his love for her shining through in every tear.

A short while later, I also experienced the loss of my Aunt Jewell, my father's sister. Despite living in Kentucky throughout her entire life, she maintained a close relationship with me, my brother, and my sister. During the summers of my childhood, she treated us like her own children, with swimming pool visits each time she came home to visit her own mom and dad. Rick had only met her once when we received the devastating news of her early death in that very same month. Diabetes had claimed her life at the young age of 46. It seemed that the experience of "loss" would be a recurring theme in our young adult lives.

Rick's family often called him "Ricky," and during the early months of our dating, I asked him what he preferred to be called (as I had known him as Bert in high school). He told me to call him "Rick," and so that became his name to me. We continued to date regularly for the next eight months, and in August 1976, he asked me to marry him. It was one of the happiest days of my life. We decided to plan our wedding for November because we both felt ready for marriage. The arrangements came together smoothly, and on November 6, 1976, we exchanged vows at the Brush Creek Presbyterian Church in Ridgeview, WV, the same little church I attended as a young child. Although it wasn't the church I attended during my teen years, we felt it would be a good place to begin our married life since my parents were still members there. Reverend Harry Palmer, a wise and insightful man, provided us with counseling and officiated our wedding. He became like family to us over the next several years. I was 23 years old, and Rick was 25 when we tied the knot.

While we were searching for a suitable location to build our house, tragedy struck our young lives. One day, when I was expecting our second child, my father-in-law called and asked if I could pick up Rick's sister's children from school. It was an unusual request, as Grandpa Peros typically handled that responsibility. He had been working next door with a neighbor, overseeing the plumbing and installation of a septic system. Due to his history of heart disease, he mostly sat in a chair and instructed them on what to do while the work was being done. Upon returning to their house after picking up the kids in Charleston, we received the devastating news that Grandpa had passed away while sitting in my neighbor's yard on that hot afternoon. The following weeks were filled with profound grief that affected the entire family. Grandpa was a kind and generous man who had many friends, so his loss was deeply felt. We learned valuable lessons during those early years, one of which was that grief has no timeline; but it often continues for many years. Rick's mom particularly struggled with the death of her husband, leading to a period of difficult years for her.

We made various plans during those early years and both of us worked diligently. However, we soon realized that plans require financial resources. Working the midnight shift exhausted even the youngest man. Therefore, we pursued our plans as our budget allowed. Our first child, Jennifer Renee, was born in 1977, followed by our second child, Kristen Lea, in 1979. In 1980, Rick, Carmel, Poochie, Jim, Eddie, and several others generously assisted in constructing our home. Meanwhile, I cooked for the building crews and took care of our two young children. Rick, who worked the midnight shift, managed to squeeze in moments for working on the house before driving back to his job in the mines. Finally, we were able to move into our new home when Kris turned two years old. Countless cherished memories were made in that house, which was built with remarkable skill and filled with love.

We first lived in an apartment as a couple, then moved to the house where I was raised, nestled in a small rural hollow between the mountains, before finally completing our new home. Despite occasional blizzards that would trap and isolate us worse than on the prairie, those were the best days of our lives. On our new property, he built a treehouse and set up a large above-ground pool where the kids learned to swim, and even our nieces and nephews joined in. One year, during deep snows and cold temperatures, they even built an igloo in the front yard! Rick's vision for our lives, along with his knowledge, strength, skills, and abilities, were truly awe-inspiring as we embarked on camping trips and traveled during those early years. We felt immensely blessed by God, and our happiness knew no bounds.

I often wonder, if I had known what the future held, how much more I would have cherished and enjoyed those seemingly difficult days. There were moments of loneliness when I would spend extended periods somewhat isolated with the kids while Rick worked night shifts. During his layoffs as an electrician in the coal mines, he would take on household responsibilities, and I would return to work until his job stabilized. It was always a collaborative effort, and we shared each day with an intense love for our family and each other as spouses. In retrospect, I came to realize just how much God protected us during those challenging times.

****

(Our lives were surrounded in happiness as God fulfilled the scriptures read at our wedding: "Blessed is every one that feareth the Lord; that walketh in his ways." Psalm 128:1)

Chapter 3

Challenges Begin

Rick had a deep passion for gardening, which inspired me to learn how to pressure can and store vegetables. It was a challenging task, but the fruits of our labor were abundant. Rick's dedication to our home was just as strong as his commitment to his job. Before we got married, he had attempted to be a teacher at an electronics trade school, but speaking in front of groups filled him with dread. He would even experience physical illness each morning, vomiting from the anxiety. Eventually, he realized that his true calling was to apply his knowledge and skills in electronics and math within the industrial sector. He was a man who thrived when working with his hands.

During the early 1970s, the mining industry was experiencing a significant boom, and Rick's military background and skills were in high demand for electrical and maintenance work on underground mining equipment. However, not all mines were equally safe for underground work. There was one particular coal mine where the men had to crawl due to the low ceiling, and some even had to 'duck walk' to navigate the tight space. On the other hand, other mines had heights of 8 feet or more and utilized advanced mining equipment, with hydraulic systems as the primary production method. For the first twelve years of our marriage, Rick worked the midnight shift (11 pm-7 am), which meant I had to take on the role of both mom and dad for the majority of the week, including many weekends. During the first four years of our daughters' lives, I didn't work outside the home unless Rick was temporarily laid off due to declines in the coal industry. Nevertheless, he always provided for us and was a dedicated, hardworking individual.

Much of my childhood was overshadowed by the fear of losing either of my parents to severe health issues. They battled serious diseases and rarely visited doctors, except when faced with tragic outcomes that required significant surgeries. Despite their intermittent illnesses, they managed to work diligently throughout those years. However, when illness struck, it was always a matter of great concern. The same held true for Rick's father, who had been afflicted with severe heart disease since a young age. Thus, both of us were familiar with the emotional and financial roller coaster that families go through due to critical illnesses. As a result, neither of us consumed alcohol or smoked; we prioritized nutritious meals, and Rick maintained a consistent exercise routine. Our children's and our own well-being always revolved around maintaining good health during those early years. Rick was in excellent health and full of vitality when we first got married. Our newly completed home was a beautiful manifestation of Rick's and my shared dreams.

It was during this period, while I was at home caring for my toddlers, that doors of opportunity opened for me to pursue higher education and obtain advanced degrees. However, the available programs were quite limited at that time. Since I already held a registered nurse license, I was able to take advantage of the educational opportunities that came my way. Throughout the years, Rick supported me in attending school, allowing me to complete two additional bachelor's degrees, 45 credit hours beyond my master's degree, and obtain national certification in school nursing. Little did we know that this would prepare me for a career in school nursing that would later provide us with stability during times when Rick was seriously ill or unable to work. Some days I would report to work 7 am, work all day until 2 pm; travel to West Virginia University for evening class, drive 3 1/2 -4 hours home the same day, and back to work 7 am the next morning. It was the only way to obtain the classes needed.

That is a brief introduction to the early stages of our life, but after a few years, our journey was about to take an abrupt and unexpected turn without any indication or warning.

It is important to note that while Rick was a man of good character and had a strong moral upbringing, he did not profess to be a Christian during the first twelve years of our marriage. I prayed earnestly, lifting him up before the Lord, asking for His protective hedge as Rick traveled to his distant jobs and worked in the dangerous profession he had chosen. Although Rick accompanied me to church regularly and ensured that our daughters attended every Sunday, he had not yet surrendered his life to Jesus. This weighed heavily on me emotionally and spiritually because I believed he was very close to accepting salvation before we got married. Throughout all those years, this was a significant source of anxiety for me, but I held onto the belief that God had a plan for each of our lives, so I continued to pray.

After 12 years of prayers and seeking God's will on how to witness to Rick regarding his soul's salvation, a special revival service was held at Ashford Church of God Holiness near our home. Rick attended as many of the services as possible that week, and conviction gripped his soul. Today, many do not talk about the spiritual condition of souls, but it is crucial for eternity. On the final day of revival, a Sunday morning, with the sun pouring through the stained glass windows of the church, a song was being sung, and the Spirit of the Lord was felt by all in attendance. It was like a gentle wave on the hearts of each person there. I quietly left my place behind our pew and went to the back. I desired this moment to speak more deeply to Rick's heart without causing any disturbance. As people stood and sang, Rick rose from his seat, walked to the altar, knelt, and prayed for forgiveness and salvation to accept Jesus as his personal Savior. It was a time of celebration, and many were filled with excitement, raising their voices in praise during that precious service. This became a turning point for us as a couple and for Rick as an individual. However, we did not realize that he would face the most difficult years of his existence in the following years. Looking back, I see how God orchestrated every second. I implore you, dear soul, as you read this story, to recognize that God is in control.

During all of our years as a family, we experienced tragic illnesses affecting various members, as well as the loss of loved ones. However, we also had periods of respite when we could take breaks and enjoy vacations, bringing a sense of normalcy back into our lives, if only for a while. Once the girls were both in school, I made the decision to return to work full time as a school nurse.

Shortly after the beginning of 1989, I asked my eight-year-old daughter, Kristen, to go next door and invite my grandma to have dinner with us that evening. Kristen returned home with news that Mamaw wouldn't answer the door. I rushed over, only to find the door locked. I had to seek assistance to force it open. To my shock and dismay, I discovered her lifeless body slumped beside a gas heater. She had been leaning to regulate the flame. Despite our attempts to perform CPR, it was too late. Mamaw had passed away peacefully and unexpectedly, just moments before our arrival. She had been one of the dearest people in my life, someone who had spent many nights at my home. The devastation in my heart was indescribable.

A few years later, I was driving home from school with one of my girls and my niece who lived next door. Our kids were like brothers and sisters. As I approached my house, I noticed my mother standing on the front porch. She hollered to me, mentioning that she had worked a half day as a substitute teacher and had come home to have a really good time talking to my dad. She had slipped off into a nap and upon awakening, realized that my dad was nowhere to be found. She had called out for him, but he didn't respond. Uncertain of his whereabouts, she sought my assistance.

At that moment, I glanced behind the house (hidden from my mother's view but visible from my car) and saw my dad lying face down on the ground. A sense of urgency washed over me, and I quickly instructed the teenagers to take my mother inside while I rushed to my dad's side. I found him in an area where he had been picking grapes, surrounded by yellow jackets on that crisp autumn afternoon in

September. Without knowing whether he had been stung or was experiencing a heart-related issue, I proceeded to drag his limp body several feet to a level spot in the yard. Within seconds, I initiated CPR. It's worth noting that he had consumed coffee before the incident. The smell of coffee, combined with the atmosphere of the autumn day and fallen leaves, will forever remind me of that moment - a scar that will forever stay.

I instructed the kids to call 911, and my mother, overwhelmed with worry, was almost collapsing inside the house. However, my entire focus remained on trying to revive my dad. A volunteer fireman, who happened to be a close friend of my dad, arrived at the scene but was too distraught to assist immediately. It was a time when training volunteers in medical procedures wasn't common practice. Nevertheless, his presence offered some comfort. The wait for the ambulance felt excruciatingly long as we lived quite a distance away from the dispatch center. Exhaustion began to take its toll on me. I prayed the entire time that I worked to revive him.

When the EMTs finally arrived, they took over the resuscitation efforts. I was asked to ride up front in the ambulance. Around 10 minutes into the ride, while they continued their attempts to revive my dad, they asked me which hospital I wanted him to be taken to. My shocked mind struggled to make a decision. If there was no sign of life, I told them to head to the local hospital. However, if there was still hope, I instructed them to go towards Charleston, where his specialists were based. As we reached an intersection, the ambulance turned towards the nearest local hospital. By that point, they had been working on my dad for several minutes without any response, erasing any sense of denial that remained in my mind at that moment.

Rick and my brother Jim were working their evening shift underground in the mines that day. One thing a miner's wife never does is upset the miner while he is working underground. The fear is that if the miner gets upset, they might not be able to leave the job or be transported by buggy to the outside entry of the mine in a safe manner. When the hospital staff escorted me to the hospital chapel and asked me who to contact in the family, I told them to reach out to the mine foreman and inform them that my dad was in critical condition. I specifically asked them not to mention that he had died, but to request their immediate presence.

In the meantime, a close friend of our family, Delores Cook, picked up my mother after I called my sister-in-law and instructed her to send mom to the hospital. Delores brought her to the hospital, while I remained in the chapel. I was unable to function properly due to low blood sugar and the emotional shock. I couldn't revive my dad, and at that moment, I had so many unanswered questions. I found myself rocking back and forth in a chair, crying in shock. My sister was also informed during the crisis, but I was not functional enough to do anything at that moment. I remember staring at a lamp and receiving juice and crackers from a nurse. Much of the following hours remain a blank in my memory; shock can be cruel to the mind. When my mom arrived, she wanted to see him, but he was still intubated and had already been declared dead. At that point, I didn't want to see him. My mom collapsed and was admitted to the emergency room due to extremely high blood pressure. I was worried I might lose her too. I prayed that I would survive those moments without having a heart attack or stroke. After they treated her, they released her into our care.

My mom was unable to cope with the loss of my father. She continued to substitute teach to avoid being alone in the house, and every night, she would come to my house after dark. For six weeks, she couldn't bear to be alone in the house, no matter how hard she tried. She closed the curtains in the kitchen that provided a view of the tiny vineyard where dad was found that day. She was frightened at night, always believing that someone would break in and harm her. I would call my mom every day from that day forward for over 20 years, and many days of my life were devoted to her. I didn't realize that her excessive dependence on my brother and me was detrimental to us. Our entire world revolved around trying to "fix" mom's sadness and grief. I felt guilty if I wanted a night away or attempted to go on vacation. She found it hard to let go, and I can't do without taking care of her, regardless of whether it is fair to anyone else. While teaching children at school, mom portrayed a different person. That was her life and source of happiness. Both she and my dad had battled chronic illness for 20 years before his death. As we went through the funeral, I struggled both physically and emotionally to cope. My prayer was that I would survive and be everything I needed to be for my mom.

I write these painful notes to enlighten someone who might be in the midst of a similar journey. God has provided so many resources to help individuals cope in the same situations. None of those were available to me during those years, and while there are many more available resources today, there is still work to be done in providing support and care for victims of loss, tragedy, and devastation. I leaned heavily upon my faith, and God gave me strength. However, please seek help and allow God to direct your path if life steers you on this journey. I will always bear the scars.

We live in a broken world, but please do not allow yourself to become that broken person who will not seek counseling or the help you need. God has equipped professionals to assist in these times of need, and it could possibly make a difference in prolonging your own physical and emotional health in the long run.

*****

So many times when I was at the brink of not coping with so many traumas, God would answer my prayers and pick me up, holding me in his care.

("The Lord is close to the brokenhearted and saves those who are crushed in spirit." Psalm 34:18 NIV)

Chapter 4.

The Call At Work

Early in our marriage, Rick had changed family doctors so that his doctor would be located on his way to and from his work site. There was a promising internist near Van, WV, with whom he established routine care. Rick had been experiencing some blood pressure symptoms, according to what he had shared with me, his nurse wife. He had scheduled what I believed to be a routine appointment. Little did I know, this would be my first realization that he had been keeping health-related secrets from me. He didn't want to worry me. That morning, I knew he had a doctor's appointment, but I was unaware that the doctor had planned an exercise stress test for him at the nearby small hospital. This was a significant event during those years since stress tests were not as commonplace as they are today. As I carried on with my regular duties at the school clinic, the phone suddenly rang. To my surprise, it was Rick's doctor, who happened to know me personally.

"Why didn't you come with your husband this morning? He shouldn't have come alone for this testing;" the doctor was almost scolding in his tone as he questioned why a nurse wife would not accompany her husband, who has been having chest pain. What? I assured the physician that I had no idea what he was referring to! The physician continued, stating that Rick had failed the stress test and had left the office. He would be referring him immediately to a cardiologist in Charleston, WV. Rick was 37 years old at the time. The physician informed me that Rick was advised to do nothing but rest on the couch until he underwent further testing by a cardiologist. However, the doctor seemed oblivious to the fact that Rick was completely in denial about the severity of the situation.

After being emotionally shaken to the core, I immediately feared the worst. My mind raced, and my body trembled as I felt the shock reverberate through me. Could this really be happening? Our lives were just beginning. I had spent years grappling with my father's heart disease, surgeries, and other illnesses. Rick had his own experience with his father's heart disease. Was this really happening? As I walked through my office, tears streamed down my face. I caught sight of a coworker who embraced me, offering prayers and support. In those days, stress tests were not commonly performed, and procedures like angioplasty were still new and unfamiliar. The fact that Rick, at his age, was being referred for further tests seemed incomprehensible to me.

I prayed fervently and made it a priority to speak with Rick as soon as possible. The rest of that day remains a blur, but I made sure he arrived home safely. I vaguely recall leaving work, but the drive home escapes my memory. Eventually, I managed to gather some information from him, learning that he was scheduled for a stress thallium study, also known as a nuclear stress test, on his heart within a few days. We were informed that the exercise stress test might be unreliable and further imaging of the heart would be necessary to determine the next steps. I held onto the hope that everything would turn out fine. I began praying relentlessly, unaware that those prayers would continue for the next 24 years. Yes, you read that correctly: 24 years.

As a nurse, my anxiety and fear kicked into high gear. I attempted to conceal my apprehension from Rick, but he completely withdrew emotionally from me. At that moment, an unspoken tension hung in the air, like a "secret elephant in the room." Neither Rick nor I were aware of its presence, but as our journey unfolds, you will come to understand why I describe it that way. I want to emphasize that this is a common reaction between patients and their spouses. A wide range of emotions emerges when your closest love, your soul mate, is dealt a serious blow. There is no "normal" in such situations, and striving for normalcy only adds stress to each moment. There is no script or instruction book, and even if there were, there would be no time to read it. Every moment requires vigilant attention, and as a spouse, every question that escapes your lips may be perceived as nagging, intrusive, or worse. The individual going through the health crisis typically feels isolated, believing that no one truly comprehends their experience, and in many ways, they are RIGHT. Each person is unique, and their response to the situation will differ.

Within a couple of days, I found myself anxiously waiting in the reception area of the large medical center near our home as Rick underwent the first of many tests. The stress test was an extensive procedure involving nuclear medicine injections and follow-up imaging that would take hours to complete. Before long, the cardiologist and his nurse practitioner emerged from the testing area, their expressions grave as they took seats on either side of me. I sat alone, the atmosphere heavy with tension, as they quietly delivered the news that Rick, or "Bert" as they referred to him, had failed the initial phase of the stress test. Their words seemed to reverberate loudly in my ears, causing my anxiety to intensify. My blood pressure soared as a flood of thoughts from my experiences with my father's heart disease raced through my mind.

The doctor continued, "He is in denial," he said. "His EKG showed irregularities, and we almost had to forcibly stop him from continuing on the treadmill as he kept insisting that he was fine." They informed me that Rick would be sent home for the weekend but instructed him to do nothing except rest on the couch until his return on Monday for a cardiac catheterization. If he experienced any difficulties or complaints during the weekend, I was to take him to the emergency room. Wait a minute! Here they were, explaining the seriousness of the situation and recounting how they had a man on a treadmill refusing to stop, yet now they were sending him home under strict orders to avoid physical exertion and stress until his next test? They mentioned that there was a remote possibility of the stress test being a false positive, but given that Rick had failed two stress tests, it was unlikely. The cardiac catheterization would provide definitive answers. Nowadays, with the advancements in cardiac medicine, a patient experiencing the symptoms Rick had would never be sent home. Even back then, the doctor indicated that cardiac issues at his age were generally considered life-threatening.

"My mind raced, and my blood pressure soared. I was incredibly nervous to see Rick again, and I am unable to fully express how I felt during those next three days. Rick wouldn't talk, and I started questioning myself: had I done something wrong? Had I somehow angered him? He seemed genuinely angry, and I couldn't understand what was happening. Whenever I repeated unanswered questions to him, he accused me of nagging, making me believe that I must have done something to upset him. As I tried to decipher his thoughts—because, as a wife, it's expected that I can read minds when spouses become nonverbal—I found myself in a state of physical and mental distress, mirroring the patient himself. I was constantly nervous, anxious, and unable to sleep, as the deafening silence filled our home. How could I explain the severity of the situation to our young girls? How could I convey that their dad was sitting there, staring, and not talking about anything and why this was happening?

Apparently, Rick believed there had been a serious medical mistake, and he was convinced he didn't have any heart problems. Trust me, that was my prayer as well. Finally, Monday arrived, and he was admitted to the hospital. He would undergo cardiac catheterization that day, but if the doctor deemed angioplasty with stents necessary, the procedure wouldn't be performed immediately. He would have to return to the cath lab for a second time, once an emergency backup 'open heart surgical team' was available on standby, just in case. Today, much of that has changed, and cardiac stent procedures are done simultaneously with the first catheterization.

Take a moment and imagine the whirlwind of emotions racing through both of our minds. The love of my life was facing the possibility of death (these procedures weren't common yet, and only a few skilled physicians could perform them). My husband was dealing with a life-altering heart condition at a very young age, and the only person he could relate to was his own father. However, his father's symptoms hadn't improved with open-heart surgery, and he passed away at a young age. Rick was 37, and I was 36 years old; our lives were spinning out of control in that moment. I couldn't confide in anyone because Rick was still in denial about being sick. If the phone rang, I could only have minimal discussions with our closest family members.

Although the catheterization itself only takes approximately 15-20 minutes, I would soon discover that the waiting time for families in the hot, poorly ventilated, and crowded waiting area would be 1 ½ to 2 hours. During this time, my blood pressure continued to rise, my blood sugar dropped, and I struggled to sit quietly, praying that everything would be alright. I hoped that Rick didn't have any blockages, and I feared that I might have a heart attack or stroke myself as I waited. My pulse raced at over 120 beats per minute during the wait. The emotions were overwhelming. Finally, the doctor came to the area and spoke with me. There were four blockages, one of which was located just prior to where the main vessels branch over the front wall of the heart, commonly referred to as the 'widow maker.' Thank God Rick hadn't experienced a cardiac event yet, and the doctor believed that angioplasty alone (during this time in medical history, stents were not typically placed initially) would make him fully functional within a couple of weeks, with only one week off from work. The 'work' issue was a major concern for Rick, as he was a dedicated workaholic. His procedure would be completed the following day.

As I approached Rick's bedside that evening, he remained quiet and had nothing to say. When the doctor came and spoke with him, my emotions intensified as Rick appeared angry and nonverbal. I was concerned that the doctor might perceive us as an emotionally distant couple. How could I reach Rick? What could I do? Why couldn't he understand that I was equally concerned about his well-being? At that moment, I felt physically ill and realized that if I didn't step back and go home for some brief rest, I wouldn't be able to make it through the day of the procedure. The doctor explained all the potential complications associated with the angioplasty, which was a relatively new procedure replacing open-heart grafting of the arteries. This added to the fear both the patient and their family experienced. Fortunately, the first angioplasty, scheduled for the next day, was successful. With one week off work, Rick immediately started feeling excellent. He was thrilled because the pressure and discomfort in his chest had gradually developed, and he hadn't realized it until it was gone. He felt a remarkable improvement in his overall well-being.

During those early years, I became overly protective of Rick. However, the doctor advised me to step back and allow Rick to engage in as much physical exertion as he could handle. It was reassuring to hear that his cardiac performance was excellent, and it had prevented a potentially deadly heart attack at his young age of 37. Unfortunately, after just eight short weeks, Rick began experiencing angina and had to return to the cardiologist. In some patients, the body reacts to the first angioplasty by sending scar tissue to the surgical area of the arteries, similar to how the body heals a wound. This scar tissue can cause the artery to become clogged again. Nowadays, stents are pretreated with substances to prevent this process, and patients are also prescribed medications to help prevent such complications. Additionally, stents are now commonly placed during angioplasty procedures. As anticipated, Rick required a repeat angioplasty to open the area and place a stent. These timely procedures were necessary. Unfortunately, over the next nine years, he underwent numerous cardiac catheterizations, four additional angioplasties, and routine stress tests to monitor and maintain his cardiac function. Despite the challenges, both of us continued working, and our two daughters completed high school and started their first four years of college. An important change occurred in Rick's care as he chose to transfer his basic medical management to a young internist in Charleston, WV, Dr. Jack Kinder, since he was requiring frequent hospitalizations and careful monitoring of his routine medications.

One might wonder about the spiritual and emotional journey our family went through during all those years. I had been a professing Christian for most of my life and relied heavily on my faith and prayer to help me overcome life's struggles. Rick had attended church regularly with me during the first 12 years of our marriage, but he had never felt the need for personal salvation. After all, he was a man of strong moral character and held unmatched beliefs. He attended church more often than most professing Christians and enjoyed the fellowship of ministers and missionaries who visited our home. I remember seeking guidance from every minister on how to bring Rick to Christ. Their response was usually to "love him in" and continue praying, which I faithfully did. It wasn't until the winter just before his first cardiac problems that he felt convicted to embrace salvation and become a professing Christian. During his early illness, my concern was that he would become discouraged in his faith. As I witnessed him go through the stages of grieving (shock and disbelief, anger, projection, depression, bargaining, and I wasn't entirely certain if I had ever witnessed acceptance), I prayed that he would trust God and find strength to navigate his circumstances. Rick had taken such good care of his physical health, which led him to wonder why this was happening to him while others who abused their bodies in various ways seemed to remain unaffected by health issues.

Although our family had many wonderful moments in between episodes of illness, each time Rick fell ill, he would retreat into a private world of nonverbal anger and frustration. As a practicing nurse, I had never fully learned or understood that patients have to start from stage one of the grieving process, or begin their unique journey of grief, with each traumatic episode of chronic illness. There are no shortcuts or exemptions that can shield someone from experiencing the anxiety, fear, and overwhelming emotions that come with life-threatening chronic illness. The challenging aspect is that few physicians or nurses recognize the need for emotional support during these times. We often struggled on our own during each episode, with Rick withdrawing and speaking very little. It took me a long time to realize that his behavior was not a personal attack against me. I failed to grasp, throughout all those years, that his anger was not directed at me personally. There was definitely an elephant in the room!

I would work until I was exhausted, trying to fix the right food, prepare the correct meal, make the bed just right, and take responsibilities away that might stress him more. But the reality that few spouses realize is that they cannot 'fix 'it at all! Throughout all the years of illness, very few nurses or physicians asked about the wife—the wife who felt like she was drowning in an ocean of recurring life-threatening events concerning her spouse. So, I immersed myself in new goals, achievements, education—anything I could do to make things better for us and cope with the journey we had been dealt. I prayed constantly for God's will to be done but also for my husband's healing. The emotions that first emerged when I dealt with my parents' illnesses were compounded by the genuine fear of possibly losing my Rick. I sincerely hope that counselors, pastors, or other well-meaning professionals who suggest that fear or anxiety is sinful or shows a lack of trust in God realize that such statements are not true. The human experience in these types of situations often leads to fear. Even a person with the strongest faith will inevitably experience these human emotions. My prayers persisted, moment to moment. We received many miracles over the years, for which we were profoundly grateful to God!

The next several years would be a series of crises with little normalcy scattered along the way. Although the medical world did not acknowledge the constant stress our lives endured and never addressed the emotional side, it was even more difficult because very few of our closest friends realized it. Did you truly understand what I just wrote? This went on for years without any breaks, with the looming threat of physical disaster ever-present. Friends and family were there for the crises, but nobody entered the privacy of our home and witnessed the endless days, hours, and years of emotional pain and anguish experienced by the patient with chronic illness, as well as their spouse and family. Our children look up to us and mimic our behaviors, and though we shielded them from some of the details when they were very young, our daughters were exposed to this emotional stress as young teens and into adulthood, when most kids are enjoying life and social development. It's no wonder that children in homes with this kind of trauma feel the need to be 'perfect children' to avoid causing any more pain or stress for the ill parent. As a result, the 'other parent' often experiences some of those 'normal flairs of emotion' from the children, while desperately trying to protect the 'ill' parent.

Let me digress for a moment and remind every medical professional, family member, and school teacher of children with chronically ill parents of the following: amidst the medical procedures, life-threatening events, and nightmares that these children and spouses are experiencing, the normal stresses of everyday life persist. Often, they may react or overreact to seemingly trivial things simply because they are trying to survive. Each individual's emotions are intertwined in a state of 'survival mode,' and it is crucial for school personnel, physicians, nurses, friends, and church members to comprehend this. Every time Rick returned to work, everyone believed it was finally over, but that was not the case. The chronic illness continued to progress, carrying with it a myriad of emotions.

My faith in God and experiencing His sustaining strength is something I want to emphasize at this point. I would have loathed going through these challenging times without God in my life. I truly believe I wouldn't have survived.

My faith had grown stronger, and I found myself praying for miracles every day. What I didn't realize then was that I was in training because, surprisingly, this was the least difficult period of our lives!

To summarize, during these times, family members may not realize the full range of behaviors that surround them. They may lack a reference point for what constitutes a normal life, and often, the emotions they experience differ from what is considered typical. Additionally, family members tend to avoid seeking help or seeking emotional support, particularly if they hold careers in ministry or healthcare occupations. They are so preoccupied with the survival of their loved one, time does not lend itself for the individuals to seek personal health care.   There can be various reasons for this phenomenon. One possibility is that cultural beliefs dictate that individuals in faith or health professions should not exhibit normal reactions to such traumatic situations, which can influence them to avoid seeking care or expressing their own trauma. In fact, they may have been conditioned to "tough it out and carry on" as part of their professional training. As caregivers who assist others in coping with chronic illness, they often neglect to ask for help themselves. Additionally, the overwhelming nature of their circumstances can leave them devoid of the emotional and physical energy required to seek help or counseling.

As mentioned earlier, throughout the years, there were moments when we were fortunate enough to enjoy one-week vacations, providing a glimpse of normalcy amidst the challenges. However, amidst this personal turmoil, I encountered a distressing incident: my beloved grandma collapsed, and despite our attempts at CPR, we were unsuccessful in reviving her. She had been an unwavering source of support for us, and her loss deeply affected us. Additionally, while dealing with Rick's illness, I also had to confront the tragic passing of my own father. This sequence of events highlights the varied forms in which trauma can manifest in our lives. It is likely that many who read this passage can relate to such experiences. Nevertheless, I firmly believe that God, in His omniscience, guided me through each step of my journey, equipping me with the strength to persevere and continue my mission of ministering to others. Reflecting on these years, I am amazed at how each experience served as preparation for what lay ahead.

As I witnessed my mom's grieving process over a span of 20 years, as well as the experiences of other members in Rick's family, I found it challenging to comprehend why they seemed unable to fully express their sorrow and progress forward. It took many years for me to gain the understanding I needed.

*****

("Blessed are they that mourn, for they will be comforted." Matthew 5:4 NIV)

CHAPTER 5

THE FAMILY REUNION

We were sitting under a picnic canopy on a hot June day, with the scent of chestnut bloom filling the air. I distinctly remember the chestnut bloom because it triggers my allergies, often leading to vertigo or headaches when I'm outdoors. It was my mom's family reunion, the Peters family reunion, and everyone was engaged in lively conversations, thoroughly enjoying the event. While engrossed in conversation, I unconsciously reached over and patted Rick's leg around the knee area. To my surprise, my hand recoiled as if I had struck a tightly stretched drum or a lifeless log. Curious, I asked, 'Rick, is your leg swollen?' Initially, I assumed he might have injured his knee at work or in the garden. However, he simply mentioned that he had noticed some swelling in his legs and didn't elaborate further, as we continued socializing with our relatives. My stomach sank, and I couldn't help but wonder what was happening with him. Merely six weeks prior, he had received excellent news that his routine stress test showed normal results and his heart function was excellent. So, I couldn't understand why he was experiencing this unexpected development.

That evening, as we prepared for bed, I glanced over and noticed Rick's back. I was shocked to see pitting edema above his waist; any pressure applied to his skin left a noticeable dent. Concerned, I insisted that we contact our family internist first thing in the morning. Upon consulting with Dr. Kinder, it was decided that Rick should undergo an immediate series of lab tests. Reluctantly, Rick agreed to go, although he often became upset and loathed missing work for medical appointments. The following day, after the lab tests were conducted, Dr. Kinder personally called to inform me that Rick's kidney function was diminished based on the results. He requested Rick to return for another set of labs to ascertain the cause and rule out any potential laboratory errors. This was just one of many times Dr. Kinder caught significant medical issues early on, caring for Rick as his patient in a timely manner.

A new health crisis ensued when testing failed to reveal a specific cause, and Rick was immediately referred to a nephrologist for idiopathic nephrotic syndrome, a condition characterized by kidney symptoms and altered function with no known cause. Over the next few weeks, various diseases were explored, but no answers were found. The appointments were anxiety-provoking for Rick due to the lack of answers, yet he was required to take multiple medications to balance his blood pressure, body fluids, and renal function. It's important to note that Rick was not fond of taking medications, even as simple as Tylenol or aspirin, and he was reluctant to take any unnecessary drugs. Despite his blood pressure occasionally being normal, the nephrologist added new medications typically used to lower blood pressure because they sometimes enhance kidney function.

All of this was overwhelming for Rick, and he often requested my presence at his appointments to help decipher the nephrologist's explanations, given his use of complex medical language. Eventually, he was scheduled for a kidney biopsy to determine his diagnosis, despite the risks involved, such as infection, kidney loss, and severe bleeding. We prayed for a successful procedure, and fortunately, it went well. I eagerly awaited the results and, prior to his appointment, I spoke to someone in the office who informed me that the doctor preferred to deliver the information personally. However, they sensed my anxiety as a fellow nurse and shared what the biopsy had shown. Three days later, when the nephrologist disclosed the results, it was a different diagnosis. I questioned the doctor, and he explained that there had been a lab mix-up earlier when Rick's and another patient's biopsy samples were inadvertently switched. Thankfully, the lab's error control system had identified and rectified the mistake. This revelation did not provide a great sense of relief. Now the question remained, which diagnosis was accurate? I was reassured by both the nephrologist and another physician that the treatment for either diagnosis would be the same, rendering the lab error inconsequential. They were confident that the lab error had been corrected, and the accurate diagnosis was obtained. Consequently, Rick's final diagnosis was membranous glomerulonephritis. Since obtaining kidney biopsies is not a casual procedure, we accepted this diagnosis. As soon as I had access to my computer, I began searching medical journals and literature for information on the causes, prognosis, and definitions of this condition.

Nothing seemed straightforward when it came to Rick's health. Despite working as an underground electrician in the mines, he faced numerous complications. With limited research, I discovered that Cadmium can be absorbed through the skin and potentially lead to his diagnosis. I cautiously asked him if he had ever been exposed to Cadmium during his work. However, he became upset and defensive when I inquired about environmental exposure. He explained that many people in today's world try to exploit situations for personal gain, and he didn't want his company to think he was seeking worker's compensation or a free ride. Consequently, our discussion came to an abrupt halt. Over the following years, several men in Rick's work section, as well as in other mines owned by the same company, developed renal problems. Some died as a result of renal failure, while others were subjected to long-term treatments like dialysis, chemotherapy protocols, or kidney transplants. However, when I attempted to raise the question of whether their employment exposure could be a contributing factor, the nephrologist dismissed it as the normal occurrence within the general population and unlikely to be environmentally related. I found this hard to believe then, and even more so today.

The next 16 years were filled with countless laboratory studies, resulting in Rick's veins becoming scarred from multiple venipunctures. Every blood draw became increasingly difficult and painful, even for routine testing. We lived in constant fear that renal failure and end-stage renal disease would be the next stage, and throughout those 16 years, Rick underwent numerous chemotherapy protocols aimed at slowing down or possibly achieving remission of the renal disease. These protocols often came with inhuman adverse reactions or promised harsh long-term side effects, but there were no other alternatives. It was a roller coaster of existence, with occasional periods of partial remission that we were immensely grateful for. The endless cycle of 24-hour urine tests was both tiresome and frustrating. Rick had to carry a jug to work with him and collect urine throughout the day, which was a constant inconvenience. Labs and medications consumed our lives, but Rick was willing to do anything to avoid dialysis.

Throughout this period, we stayed true to our faith, praying for healing while he underwent treatment after treatment and continued working in the mines. Laden with guilt, being the hard worker that he was, he reported to work despite being so weak that he could not carry his heavy tools back underground in the mines. His buddies would step in and help him carry the tools to various locations at his work site. He deeply appreciated those friends because he wouldn't have been able to work on many of the days he did without them. I would have named his buddies that worked alongside him, but attempting to name them all would inevitably result in missing someone's name, so I won't make an attempt. However, I know many of them and will never forget Rick's gratitude for those men who worked by his side for many years. They were like family to him. He would go to work immediately following chemotherapy treatments, take his nausea medication, and never miss a shift. He didn't talk about it with me; it was a great big elephant that lived in our house for many years.

There are no words to express how these years were filled with every intense emotion known to mankind, not just for Rick but also for myself, and at times, for our daughters. As mentioned earlier, we shielded them from certain information during their early years, but as they grew into young adults, we shared everything with them. I sometimes envied the close relationship between the girls and their father. He was wise in guiding them through long conversations, and I felt that they understood the fragility of his existence. They often had to display maturity beyond their years, during many emergencies that occurred. The girls tended to argue more with me than with their dad during those typical disagreeing "teen moments" as they were growing up. Those were precious times that I miss dearly. Most of the time, his health was a matter of life and death, with no in-between. However, he persisted in working and resisted applying for disability even with the encouragement of his doctors, especially during those earlier years. Rick attended church regularly also; never wavering in his faith. Each Sunday for Sunday school class, he presented an uplifting, thought provoking quote of the week. The class looked forward to his motivational comment at the opening of each session. Rick loved his pastors over the years and his Sunday class when Randy Nelson taught insightful lessons from the Bible, which helped Rick survive his journey.

Rick had an exceptional cardiologist and a nurse practitioner who supported him through numerous emergencies during his twenty-year battle with chronic heart illness. They genuinely loved and cared for him, just like his family internist. One of the greatest challenges arose during his treatment with high doses of steroids for the renal disease, which accelerated his arteriosclerosis by increasing his cholesterol levels and causing clogs in his stents and blood vessels. This eventually led to the need for emergency cardiac bypass surgery. His previous angioplasty procedures had sustained him until his forties, but now the major surgery he had feared was looming ahead. Each procedure or test brought the burden of worrying about additional potential kidney damage. No one knew when or if dialysis might become a permanent necessity due to exposure to various contrast dyes and medications and the cardiac surgery he was about to undergo. Immediately after his open-heart surgery, he developed pericarditis. Unfortunately, he went into renal failure after taking a single anti-inflammatory medication tablet. Through much prayer and 24 hours after discontinuing the medication, his kidneys began functioning again, and he once again avoided dialysis. I brought him home on Christmas Eve that year, just five days after his open-heart surgery.

After the expected recovery period, he returned to work. He felt immensely happy and well after his bypass surgery, but the chronic renal problems persisted. However, there were brief periods when he felt better than usual. During those times, we would take short trips or travel short distances to enjoy a brief vacation. It was during these years that Kris, our youngest daughter, was pursuing her pre-med degree at Alderson-Broaddus College in Philippi, WV, a Christian college. She was actively involved in campus Christian clubs and groups, who became our prayer warriors, alongside our home church, the Ashford Church of God (Holiness). Rick cherished the notes he received from Kris and Jenny, our oldest daughter, who was still living at home during her college years. In these notes, they would explain how many people were praying for him and his health issues and how these individuals continued to pray for his healing. We experienced many miracles during those years! When things would get so grim, God intervened and spared Rick. I never took those miracles lightly.

A couple of times, Rick experienced sepsis, which is an infection in the bloodstream resulting from infections acquired during his treatment for renal disease. The medications he took to treat his disease weakened his immune system, making him highly susceptible to infections. There was a particular incident when both girls were in college, and the doctor informed me to have them come home to see their dad as his condition appeared critical and unpredictable. I remember praying and doing my best to cope with the situation. Miraculously, he started responding to the treatment within two hours, and his renal failure reversed within 24 hours. It was evident to me that God had a purpose in sustaining Rick, and he would soon return to work once again. Rick never quit praying for total healing, nor did I.

One day we were at the CAMC Memorial Hospital/ WVU Medical School Campus, as we drove from the parking lot after a discouraging doctor's appointment. A large group of medical students were crossing the road with their white coats on, looking so professional. I will never forget how he sadly said, "I'll never see Kris like that." He meant he would never see her in her white coat. My heart sank, and I tried to speak some empty words of encouragement, but it was apparent that he felt life slipping away with all the odds he was facing with the heart and renal disease.

But he couldn't have been more wrong! Through the power of prayers, he was uplifted and experienced numerous instances where he was touched just as he reached the brink of catastrophic physical illness.

Whenever we visited new specialists and they reviewed his clinical records before meeting him, they were often puzzled. He defied the stereotypical image of a sick patient because he never "looked" the part. He was a true fighter, relentless in his pursuit of life.

Jenny completed her first four years of college with honors and became a teacher. Later on, she went beyond her initial degree and master's to specialize in reading and special education. This delighted Rick, and his goal was to work until both of his daughters finished school, providing them with as much support as possible. We were thrilled with Jenny's college completion and successful career as a teacher, and we were so proud of her. Furthermore, Rick had the privilege of attending not only Kristen's White Coat Ceremony on her journey to becoming a physician but also her Medical School Graduation and Residency awards ceremonies as a successful physician. He would get to know both girls' husbands, children, attend the birth of grandson Daniel, and got to attend court during chemotherapy, when our beloved granddaughter Lily was adopted into our hearts. Despite his illness, Rick continued to work as an electrician in the mines for all those years until he completed 30 years and retired. At the urging of his physician, he agreed to file for disability based on his end-stage renal status, a step that would take care of me someday, although neither of us had any idea at the time. Rick encouraged me to continue my education, and I went on to complete 45 credit hours beyond my master's degree, after already earning two bachelor's degrees. Eventually, I became the Director of School Health Services for the Boone County school district and retired from that position , after obtaining my National School Nurse Certification and 26 years of service. He supported me throughout.

During one of Rick's healthier periods, our family had the opportunity to travel to Disney World in Florida. It was an unforgettable experience, especially for me, as I received the honor of being named the National School Nurse of the Year in 2002 by NASN. We cherished every moment we had together during all these years. Despite the challenges we faced, we made it a priority to go on vacation with our daughters almost every summer, ensuring we spent at least a week away. Additionally, throughout the year, we often took weekend trips to Ohio Amish Country, our favorite spot. We would save up and purchase one piece of Amish furniture each year to replace something old in our home. It was a special tradition, and we enjoyed the process of shopping for these unique pieces. However, amidst all the enjoyable moments, our activities and dreams had to revolve around the demanding schedule of doctors' appointments and medical labs related to Rick's renal disease treatments. Many times, when we attempted to relax, we had pending tests or surgeries awaiting our return home. It was a constant reminder of the challenges we faced, but we did our best to make the most of our time together. Over the years I would require major surgery a couple times, with recovery, which complicated our whole scheme of things.

What many medical professionals fail to realize is that even between doctor visits, whether it's six weeks, four weeks, or any other time frame, there is always a lingering overwhelming feeling for those living with a chronic illness. It's the constant fear and anxiety of waiting for the next crisis to strike, not a matter of if, but when. During these times, prayers are offered, and the protective peace provided by God comforts both the Christian patient and their family as they continue on their journey. I often reflect on the families who lack a support system or a church community. I wonder how they cope without the sustaining power of faith. Unfortunately, many physicians and specialists overlook this aspect, and I can only imagine the heightened fear and anxiety these families must endure.

Many mornings, I would reach out and touch Rick, checking to see if he was still breathing. He often appeared restless and would experience intermittent sleep apnea throughout the night. Sometimes, he would cry like a baby in his sleep, clearly struggling with emotional stress in his dreams. However, he never shared the nightmares with me; he would only mention that they were really bad.

Despite his own challenges, Rick was grateful for each day and believed in living life to the fullest. He refused to waste his life in a perpetual state of grieving, regardless of the cause. He firmly believed that no matter how serious an offense someone may commit against you, it was essential to forgive and move forward. Rick understood that life was too fragile to be consumed by anger. While he battled some of these angers privately, he never shared the details with me, though I suspected I had some understanding. However, he consistently forgave individuals and pressed on. It took him many years to achieve this mindset; like all of us, he was a work in progress. Throughout the years, many souls were watching Rick's journey. I firmly believe that his battles, survival, and unwavering faith touched lives, inspiring others who observed his strength and resilience.

*****

("But they that wait upon the Lord shall renew their strength; they shall

    mount up with wings as eagles; they shall run, and not be weary; and they shall walk, and not faint." Isaiah 40:31 KJV)

Chapter 6

Chronic Illness and the Marital Relationship

The topic of the sexual relationship between couples facing chronic illness is rarely, if ever, discussed by the specialists attending to the patient. However, it's crucial to recognize that intimacy remains an important aspect for both husband and wife, even in the face of a life-threatening health crisis, when the illness becomes chronic. I once made a lighthearted remark to friends, joking that the "sex" chapter of my book would be the shortest, simply stating, "it was good." However, it is important to delve deeper into this subject, as the sexual aspect of a relationship can be significantly impacted by chronic illness.

Rick was a very private, loving, gentle man from the moment I met and fell in love with him. Throughout the many years of his illness, we discovered that couples facing traumatic illnesses must find alternative ways to express their love for each other. There are no set rules for married couples seeking comfort, love, and fulfillment during these critical times. Human touch, in itself, is the most healing and loving action a couple can engage in. It helps the "ill" spouse maintain a sense of normalcy and experience the love that should not be taken away. Unfortunately, our culture has limited the definition of "sex" so severely that couples often forget the most powerful tools of connection and satisfaction. It is important to remember that there is no prescribed way to fulfill each other's needs in this realm; God made us to complement and fulfill one another. Each person must continue communicating with their partner and truly listen to understand what they need for fulfillment. It is crucial to acknowledge that the illness affects both individuals, and the performance may be influenced by medications that the person needs to take. Regardless of the circumstances, it is essential not to shut out your partner in the relationship. Embrace caresses, touches, and demonstrations of love for as long as possible; it will contribute positively to the relationship. These efforts should not be underestimated, as the health condition strips the individual of their sexual identity among other things it takes away.

In November 2001, Jenny planned a surprise 25th wedding anniversary reception for us at our church, with the help of our family. It was a cherished milestone for us. However, on that day, Rick was feeling extremely sick and nauseated from a new chemotherapy treatment he had started for his renal disease. Despite his condition, he pushed through, although he couldn't even stand for me to feed him cake for pictures. I felt a deep sense of empathy for him, knowing how much he would have typically enjoyed that day. Nevertheless, Jenny did an excellent job organizing the event, and we were incredibly grateful for her efforts.

We often had to suppress the fear and anxiety of the moment to comfort one another.

*****

("For God hath not given us the spirit of fear; but of power, and of love and of a sound mind." 2 Timothy 1:7 KJV)

CHAPTER 7

THE REFERRAL

Rick had always been reluctant to entertain the idea of seeking a second opinion regarding his renal disease. However, after approximately 14 years, it became evident that his kidney function was rapidly deteriorating, as indicated by the alarming numbers reflecting his condition. Despite undergoing all the initial tests and biopsies again, no new findings emerged. Rick's nephrologist explained that he had exhausted all known treatment options documented in the medical literature. Therefore, he recommended that Rick make a six-hour journey to the University of North Carolina, Chapel Hill, for a thorough evaluation. This evaluation would determine whether there were any current medication protocols being researched for membranous glomerulonephritis and whether Rick would qualify for participation in treatment trials. The physician he would be seeing specialized in this disease and had dedicated his life to its study since 1989, a span of over two decades by 2011.

Rick followed his physician's recommendation, and for the next two years, we traveled back and forth, undergoing another series of tests and beginning a different type of chemotherapy for his treatment. During this time, we discovered that there were only two medications remaining to try. The nephrologist at UNC (University of North Carolina) explained to Rick that after thoroughly reviewing his medical records, nothing would have been done differently if he had come to UNC earlier. However, the nephrologist recommended some changes in the daily medications that Rick had been taking, as prescribed by the other nephrologist. Additionally, the UNC team requested some additional tests to ensure that Rick did not have any form of cancer because that is often the culprit that causes end-stage renal disease with Rick's diagnosis, so more tests, more stress, were ordered.

The research nephrologist at UNC did two things differently that medical professionals need to take note of, as they made a tremendous difference in Rick's attitude toward his illness at that particular time. First, he immediately assessed Rick's emotional reaction to the chronic illness that Rick had endured for so many years. The doctor truly understood Rick's situation. Rick had been making statements like, "I feel lazy all the time," and he would often have tears in his eyes with a quivering voice. The doctor pulled his seat closer to Rick's face in the clinic room, establishing a one-on-one connection and making direct eye contact. He spent around 15 minutes or more intently "listening" to Rick's description of how he felt, and he also took the time to read a summary of Rick's entire medical history, which I had prepared in a concise narrative. The doctor then expressed his surprise at seeing Rick's appearance and how much he was physically capable of doing in his garden and at work. He stated, "Mr. Peros, you are not lazy! There is nothing about you that is lazy. Your illness depletes your energy, and most people with your lab numbers are unable to function at all."

The other significant difference with this doctor was that he engaged in direct conversation with Rick, the patient. I observed, alongside the medical resident physicians in the room, feeling like a fly on the wall. Unlike the past specialists who primarily communicated with the "nurse and wife" present in the room, this doctor restored Rick's sense of human dignity and decision-making power by speaking directly to him. It was a similar relationship and communication style that Rick's internist, Dr. Kinder, had always maintained, and he appreciated that the specialists in this unfamiliar setting treated him with the same level of respect.

The researcher provided a glimmer of hope during a time when Rick felt utterly hopeless. He proposed trying two additional protocols in an effort to achieve remission of this dreadful disease, if possible. The first option was ACTH, a growth hormone that had shown success in 75% of patients in England who had the same diagnosis. Rick agreed to this treatment as it seemed to have fewer side effects compared to many of the drugs he had previously tried. The administration would involve injections, and I would have the ability to administer it at home.

At first, he was on a low dose and everything was fine. We returned to UNC months later for a follow-up, and there was minimal improvement, but at least he hadn't worsened. So the doctors decided to increase the dosage. Within a couple of weeks, it became apparent to me that there was a serious problem. Rick began experiencing mood swings. One minute, he would act like Superman, gardening and completing tasks with an incredible amount of energy. It was as if a team of men had been working on the property all day when I came home from work, with all the tasks completed. However, about four days after the injections, he became extremely unpredictable. It took me a while to realize that this was not just my imagination. He started saying things he had never said before, especially in response to topics we discussed. He became angry and responded harshly. It was clearly a nightmare for me, and he was struggling emotionally because he couldn't control these outbursts. I would cry and wonder what to do, still not connecting the cause to the medication he was taking for his kidney disease.

Then, I noticed a pattern in how these outbursts and depressive episodes were occurring. I contacted the doctor, and he scheduled a follow-up visit to UNC for the next week to assess Rick's condition. The doctors listened carefully as I explained the issue we were facing. I pretended that I needed to use the restroom and spoke with the nurse in the hallway. I shared my suspicion that the medication was affecting Rick's brain, and I probably couldn't discuss it in front of him without upsetting him. To my surprise, when the doctor entered the room, Rick immediately started expressing his frustration, how difficult he had become to live with, and how these outbursts were beyond his control. The physician quickly realized that the ACTH dosage needed adjustment, and suggested two injections per week instead of one.

"We returned home and started the new dosage, and the problems disappeared immediately. As new issues continued to arise regularly, we prayed fervently for a miracle. Rick felt conflicted and puzzled about why he, who had lived a moral, Christian life, was suffering while individuals he knew, who lived wickedly, seemed healthy and fine. In these terribly difficult days, he learned to lean on the Lord for support. It was a hard truth for him to accept that being wholesome and good didn't guarantee a smooth journey through life - a bitter pill to swallow!"

"After an extended period on the medication, it was determined that Rick was experiencing further loss of renal function, and additional measures were necessary to preserve his kidney function. There was only one other medication available, but it came with alarming potential side effects. On one hand, it offered hope for remission of his illness, but on the other hand, it carried the risk of a fatal brain virus. Once again, as the roller coaster of this dreaded illness had shown over the years, there were no other options on the table. After several weeks of seeking approval for the experimental drug and arranging for its transportation to an infusion center in Charleston, WV, the staff at UNC conducted baseline labs and sent us home to await the first appointment for Rick to receive the drug.

While we waited for the first appointment, it was time for Rick to visit Dr. Kinder for his annual physical examination. Neither Rick nor I could have anticipated the dramatic turn life was about to take, despite everything we had experienced during the many years of his illness."

*****

("Rest in the Lord, and wait patiently for him; fret not thyself because of him who prospereth in his way, because of the man who bringeth wicked devices to pass." Psalm 37: 7 KJV)

CHAPTER 8

A Cruel Turn of Events

After Rick's visits to UNC, the doctors would forward his latest lab results to myself and his nephrologist since I liked to monitor his progress. His last lab report, drawn as we were leaving Chapel Hill, indicated an outrageous drop in his white blood cell count, so much and so out of character for his routine labs that the doctors at UNC felt it surely was a lab error and did not even give it due credence. When Rick visited Dr. Kinder, for his routine labs, the same concerning result appeared. When Dr. Kinder called, I retrieved the lab report from UNC that was taken a couple of days earlier, and it confirmed that the white count had decreased even more. Dr. Kinder asked Rick to return the next day for a repeat of the labs to rule out any potential lab errors. Soon after the recheck, we received an immediate call informing us that Rick's white blood count had dropped further within just 24 hours. Dr. Kinder wasted no time and immediately referred him to a hematologist/oncologist at the local Cancer Center.

Within a few days, Rick was scheduled for a bone marrow test, which had to be repeated quickly due to confusion regarding the diagnosis on the first report. The final diagnosis revealed that he had APL, an aggressive form of leukemia. Difficult words were heard during those oncology visits. Rick was presented with two options —to receive immediate treatment by being admitted to the hospital that day and starting harsh chemotherapy, which carried the risk of further damaging his renal function and could potentially force him into dialysis; or to refuse treatment and face the prospect of dying within 6-8 weeks. Rick, being someone who cherished life, made the decision to be admitted that day and commence chemotherapy.

The cause of his leukemia was likely a result of the various treatments he had undergone over the years in his attempt to preserve his kidney function.

Unlike some other cancer protocols, leukemia treatment often involves some of the harshest and most intensive therapies available. After consulting with experts in the field, it was decided to adjust the dosages of the treatment according to Rick's renal function, aiming to achieve remission of the leukemia with reduced dosing. The initial days of treatment went relatively well, with Rick responding positively and even showing signs of improved renal function during the hydration phases when he received additional IV fluids. However, once he returned home, the next year and a half would be dedicated to progressing through the rigorous chemical protocol.

During this time, Rick had to take over 40 pills daily to balance his renal function, blood pressure, prevent fungal, viral, and bacterial infections, along with additional oral chemotherapy. I was told by the doctors that I should not "handle" the medications but pour them in a lid or cup for him, since the medications were so toxic. The medications altered his taste buds, resulting in him resorting to pouring hot sauce on everything and eating hot banana peppers to mask the unpleasant taste. Sweet things tasted sour, and sour things tasted sweet, causing him to lose his appetite for foods he used to enjoy. As a couple, we had always appreciated exploring different foods and trying out new recipes, but this experience presented a significant challenge.

After several months, it was determined that Rick had achieved remission, and our spirits soared with joy. It had been an incredibly long journey since the start, and seeing the lab results confirming REMISSION was a tremendous relief and cause for celebration.

I would like you to take a moment and go back to when he first started visiting the David Lee Cancer Center in Charleston, which was located 45 minutes away from our home. Sitting in that waiting area, especially for the first time, is something I will never forget. As I looked around, we started recognizing familiar faces from previous visits. We often wondered about the diagnoses of different individuals, especially the very young ones who had no one accompanying them for their office visit. The atmosphere was filled with sickness; few people talked, some were unable to smile, while others never lost their joy and freely smiled and talked. It was not uncommon to see individuals staring at the floor as they awaited their visit, uncertain of what news they would hear each time.

I couldn't help but notice that my mind started thinking, "Surely they must be sicker than Rick. He will get better soon." Another thought that crossed my mind was, "Should I initiate a conversation, or would they initiate it if they wanted to talk?" Do people tend to withdraw when they receive the dreaded cancer diagnosis, or do they each react differently, possibly in more positive ways? My thoughts became scattered as I contemplated, "What if one day it's me sitting here for treatment?" The most challenging moments arose when I unexpectedly encountered people I knew personally, unaware of their cancer diagnosis. Perhaps they preferred to keep it private? Should I approach them? It was the most uncomfortable and emotionally demanding waiting area I had ever experienced, with my emotions running wild. Sometimes, panic and anxiety would overpower me, causing my blood sugar to drop or forcing me to urgently head to the restroom due to stomach symptoms. I made an effort to conceal these struggles from Rick, but he was so deeply immersed in his own emotional battle and physical illness that he likely didn't notice as much.

One day, I met a lady whom we had seen in the waiting area numerous times. She always smiled and would talk freely about how she had the worst form of leukemia, AML, and how they had tried all available protocols. She laughed as we became acquainted, and we exchanged phone numbers when I learned she had no children. The last time I saw her in the visiting area, she told me that the doctor wanted to send her to MD Anderson Cancer Center in Texas for assessment regarding a new protocol. She mentioned that she was 'afraid to fly!' and laughed, recounting her family's response of "how crazy is that? You're dying but afraid to fly!!!—What can happen?" She chuckled, and I smiled. It struck me how differently she talked about death compared to anyone I had known.

A few months later, I realized why no one talks or becomes acquainted in that room. I called and learned that she had deteriorated significantly, and later I saw her obituary in the local newspaper. It hit me like a ton of bricks. While many patients survive and progress is being made, some patients do not survive. Some of the patients I've encountered have regained their health, and I knew this from my experience as a nurse. However, now I was learning it from the perspective of a wife. It made me question how I would process it in real life.

We regularly reported for Rick's lab visits, often spending 8-12 hours away from home to check in at the hospital for transfusions. We would arrive back home feeling exhausted and would attempt to cook something to eat. Eating out became difficult and sometimes dangerous for Rick due to his dangerously low blood counts and compromised immunity. As the journey progressed, we grew increasingly tired. However, there is one day that I will always remember. I was sitting for long hours, anxiously awaiting the doctors' rounds and hoping for an update while Rick was admitted. On that day, his oncologist met me in the kitchen area of the hospital floor and said, "Take care of yourself; this is a roller coaster ride, not just a trip. It is a journey." Sometimes the medical team chose not to disclose everything they had to do for treatment to the patient, as it would have been too overwhelming.

During each hospital admission for his challenging illnesses over the course of 20 years, I rarely felt like a nurse. It wasn't about confidence in myself or anyone else; it was about my husband, my love, who was so sick. I prayed and had faith, but I couldn't deny that my personality was far from calm. I always felt anxious, to the point of becoming physically ill, whenever I knew he was facing another hospitalization, ER visit, physician visit, transfusion, or any other medical procedure. His pain became my pain, and I knew deep down that he never fully understood that.

Despite everything, I continued working as a full-time school nurse coordinator and fulfilled my role as a mother, attending to the needs of my daughters whenever necessary. I would rush to the grocery store while he was receiving treatments or transfusions. I even injured myself while pulling and tugging on heavy wheelchairs that we borrowed when he was too weak to walk to medical offices or labs. There was one day when he expressed anger upon my return with a lightweight transfer wheelchair that I had purchased. It was easier for me to handle when placing it in the car. That day, the nurse was understaffed, and he experienced an episode of bowel incontinence while waiting for assistance to the restroom. He was deeply embarrassed and furious when I arrived to pick him up. I had clean clothing with me and assisted him, all the while afraid he would collapse in the hot restroom as we tried to clean him and get ready to travel home. I had groceries in the car, a 45-minute drive ahead of us, and I was feeling light-headed from low blood sugar because I hadn't taken a break, rested, or eaten properly for weeks. On top of that, I continued receiving calls from work, as things were unstable and needed my input.

In that moment, he was the weakest I had ever seen him, and that terrified me to the core. It drove me closer to God, and I fervently prayed for healing if it was God's will.

Weeks later, Rick regained his strength and no longer needed the wheelchair; someone was visiting our home, and he began telling them how great that transfer chair was when he needed it. I nearly spewed as I recalled the fight and silence I experienced with him the day I brought it to pick him up. Bahaha, and yes, I reminded him because I was human, too. To him, the wheelchair symbolized giving up independence and being able to function normally. To me, it was getting him from one place to another without him shuffling, staggering, and falling from weakness. He would regain some health after that time, however.

During the time Rick was in remission, his mother became more physically disabled and unable to care for herself properly. Due to illness in her children's families at the time, she had to be admitted to a care facility for her care. I visited her regularly and kept her updated on Rick's chemotherapy. I had a phone conversation with her one evening, and she sounded joyful as she described the gospel singing happening at her facility. However, the next morning, I received an early phone call informing me that she was being transported to the hospital. She had suffered a cardiac event and it was clear she wouldn't survive. Despite Rick's critically low blood counts, we went to the hospital, but she was already in a coma. She passed very quickly, adding to the weight of another loss in our lives. During her visitation and funeral, I couldn't help but worry about Rick as he interacted with people. I feared that he might contract a simple infection that his weakened immune system couldn't withstand. Thankfully, he remained fine, but the stress of those days took a toll on me. I ended up developing shingles, a painful condition due to the overwhelming pressure and anxiety. Nevertheless, through it all, we found strength in God's grace.

*****

("And this is the confidence that we have in him, that, if we ask anything according to his will he heareth us;" 1 John 5: 14)

"I will lift up mine eyes unto the hills, from whence cometh my help. My help cometh from the Lord, which made heaven and earth."

Psalms 121: 1,2 KJV)

Chapter 9

A Friend Closer Than A Brother

I had a wonderful friend who assisted me in cleaning and keeping the home ready during the times when we had frequent appointments or hospital admissions. Her help was an immense support, and I was grateful for her presence. In addition to her practical help, I knew that she prayed for us incessantly, offering her prayers without ceasing.

My brother, Jim, despite working full-time and having the responsibility of maintaining our mother's property as well as his own, would always lend us a hand during crises. He would collect produce from the garden or help us with whatever we needed. My sister-in-law, Nancy, who also had a demanding full-time job with long commutes, would often surprise me with tasks completed that I was too exhausted to handle myself. She even made sure my laundry was done. I was truly grateful for their support. My mother would frequently prepare a stabilizing evening meal for me. I would grab a plate, head home, and try to quickly eat before making a final call to the nurses' station. After that, I would shower and try to get some rest, although the nights were often short with little sleep. The next day, I would return to the hospital. Sometimes, I had to go to work to complete certain tasks or address emergencies before heading back to the hospital.

Nancy would attend church services and take detailed notes about the sermon, testimonies, and prayer requests. She would send these notes to Rick when he couldn't attend, ensuring he remained connected to our church community. Although my sister, Pam, and brother-in-law, Mike, lived far away and battled their own illnesses, they would frequently call and send cards to let us know they cared. We were also blessed with friends from Rick's workplace who would unexpectedly show up with a load of cut wood for the fireplace, providing warmth and comfort during those difficult times. Many friends from our church community prayed continuously throughout the years of his illness. God's presence and comforting touch were evident in the various ways we were supported and uplifted.

Once again, there were numerous friends who visited us regularly, and if I were to attempt to name them all, I would undoubtedly fail. We were blessed with spiritual mentors, prayer warriors, and friends who fervently prayed for us, hoping for miracles along our journey. There were moments when Rick would have sepsis, multiple hospitalizations, and situations that seemed bleak, but miraculously, he would recover. These instances of healing felt like divine interventions.

I prayed ceaselessly—for Rick's healing, for my own strength to endure the emotional trauma of witnessing his suffering, and for the understanding to accept his emotional withdrawal during critical illness. As mentioned before, I was often exhausted, juggling the physical and emotional stress of raising our daughters, providing them with emotional support, managing my job, and taking care of Rick's every need. The toll on my own health and the lack of sleep were undeniable.

At times, I felt judged by some when I couldn't attend church with Rick due to these overwhelming responsibilities. Nevertheless, I did everything within my power, finding solace in a spot at home where I would often face the wall, curl up in a fetal position, and pray fervently for wisdom, guidance, and protection as our journey continued. It was during those years that I truly grasped the concept of relying entirely on God. And in my reliance, I discovered that God never failed me. He bestowed countless miracles upon Rick and granted him extended years of life.

One friend, Mitch Woodrum, took him deer hunting, fishing and all the things that guys love to do, for years. Yes, not days, weeks, or even months, but for years! I had very few conversations with Mitch over the years, although we knew each other from childhood. But Rick and Mitch shared conversations that no one else was included in, nor would they ever be. The confidence and bond was unmatched. Mitch was his sounding board and vice versa I suppose. I would stay in the back of the house on early Saturday mornings and give them privacy as they shared their regular breakfast meals and talked about what troubled them that week.

The smell of fried onions and hot peppers mixed with eggs made me feel nauseated as I tried to turn over and nap. Mitch would bring deer meat to Rick during hunting trips when he was too weak to hunt himself. Rick always longed for one more deer so he could enjoy his favorite jerky or meat. However, the strong smell of the curing process and liquid smoke permeated our house during the hunting season. It made me consider the need for people to actually have dedicated "smoke houses" for that purpose. On the other hand, Rick relished the trout meals they would have when they caught fish in their favorite spot, Cherry River.

During critical moments when Rick's condition worsened, Mitch would be occupied with work and had little time to spare. There were occasions when the doctors needed to perform emergency procedures on Rick, leaving me unable to leave and get a meal. It was precisely during those high-stress times when my blood sugar would drop, that M.W. would show up with perfectly timed meals for me. His thoughtfulness allowed me to keep functioning amidst the chaos. His prayers for us were ceaseless, and his presence brought me strength when he came by.

Sometimes Rick would get somewhat bored. A favorite story is about my brother starting in the egg business. He had gotten new hens and was excited and waiting for the first eggs. While my brother was at work, Rick would boil store-bought eggs, take them, and place them in the nests. My brother would brag all evening at dinner about how many eggs those chickens were already producing! After he and Nancy had enough eggs saved, they invited their children for a big evening feast; they would enjoy the fresh eggs those dynamic chickens were laying! All was good until everyone was gathering for dinner, and Nancy started cracking the eggs! The eggs were solid, boiled eggs. It took a while, but my brother figured out that Rick had been secretly putting boiled eggs in the nests! Oh my, that was the loudest I have ever heard Rick laugh in a while!

Another time, Nancy had a dog named Max. She had gotten him at the shelter. Rick got an ad in the mail that prospective students at an online university could fill out for an enrollment packet. He filled it out, honestly answering all the questions for Max Turley (the dog). One of the questions was: do you require assistance and tutoring with your studies? Of course, he answered 'yes.' A few days later, Nancy picked up the mail, and a large enrollment packet arrived for Max Turley. Rick started laughing at dinner that night as she was going on and on about Max getting an enrollment packet for college. Those were good times!

Do you see the pattern? Our Christian friends and family carried us in prayer as we journeyed through the storm of life. Do not ever feel that you can do it alone; God did not mean for us to be alone in the storm.

("A friend loveth at all times, and a brother is born for adversity." Proverbs 17:17 KJV)

Chapter 10

The Special Christmas

Rick had been in remission for a short time when our youngest daughter, Kristen, and her husband, Paul, asked if we could stay overnight on Christmas Eve and watch the grandkids, Lily and Daniel, open presents the next morning. Rick wanted to stay, so we agreed. Although he had been feeling unwell that week, he cherished every moment of joy he could find, especially when spending time with the kids. It turned out to be a wonderful time filled with more Christmas joy than ever before that year! We were grateful for God's help and hopeful that things would continue to improve. From a distance, I couldn't help but wonder if it would be our last Christmas together. However, I quickly diverted my thoughts and tried to hold back tears as I whispered a prayer for his healing.

Those were the moments of pure happiness when the kids stayed with us or when we stayed with them. Rick longed to share experiences with his grandkids, but time was slipping away. He faced struggles over the next few months, yet he managed to sow tomato seeds in his greenhouse and nurture them. He planted nearly 200 tomato plants for his extensive garden, tended to his blackberries, went fishing occasionally, and did whatever he could muster the strength to do. Throughout this period, he relied heavily on support from his fellow

Christian brothers, seeking their counsel and praying together while I was at work.

In January, his white blood count began to decline again, leading to several weeks of testing. The test markers for leukemia, however, were coming back clear. This indicated that he was experiencing a viral infection and that his counts should eventually recover. We lived through tense days, with me continuing to work while we eagerly awaited every lab result. During his remission, the nephrologist had determined that he needed surgery to place a fistula for dialysis, as his renal function did not appear to improve. It typically takes around 6 months for the fistula to mature for use during dialysis. We often discussed the type of dialysis he would prefer if it came to that point, including the possibility of having dialysis at home. I was very fearful of such a decision, as it meant being far away from the hospital. I researched all the possibilities of different types of dialysis, trying to find a way to ensure his quality of life. At one point, Rick met with the dialysis nurse as the time seemed to draw nearer. On that particular day, I made a very emotional and difficult decision to work at school, instead of accompanying him. He tended to let me do the talking, and I felt it was important for him to engage in the conversation without my presence. Though it was a challenging choice for me, I knew it had to be his decision to make.

He told me that he spent over an hour in the room with the lady, engaged in an argument. He was angry, and she allowed him to express his anger even towards her that day. Just as he was about to tell her she didn't understand, she revealed to him that she was on dialysis herself!

It was a BREAKTHROUGH moment, realizing that someone else was also struggling with the same emotions, anger, trials, and disbelief. He made significant progress that day. I realized that God knew what He was doing when He impressed upon me not to be present during that visit. It was crucial for Rick to vocalize what he had silently carried for so many years.

During the next months, he required dialysis fistula surgery. It collapsed, so he had another surgery. My heart raced each time he had anesthesia because he had so much physically wrong. Each time he recovered, I thanked God and prayed for healing every day.

Many people have dialysis and continue with their lives normally for many years. Rick never could get to that point; he felt that somehow everything he had tried to accomplish with his health and life would be snatched away if he had to have dialysis. I have so much appreciation for those who have this struggle every day and hope a transplant is an option soon for them! Once Rick had leukemia, he was told that he would never be considered for kidney transplantation because the drugs to prevent rejection of the transplant could render him with leukemia once again. That was a critically changing statement made by the doctor that affected Rick's many outcomes from that point forward. But he never quit believing and praying for a miracle.... nor would I and many of his Christian friends.

Many times I had to stay home from church just to lie down and escape all the emotion and worry. Rick attended every possible church service he could attend, and friends would share his testimony with me. He experienced hard spiritual lessons during the years, like, good guys do have bad things happen, that it does not mean you have sinned or done wrong if you are chronically ill. He finally learned that true happiness did not have to be a total cure; that you could live life with what cards you had been dealt and enjoy the moments that are good. He prayed for others and rejoiced for others' miracles. And he praised God not only in the storm of life but for each miracle he was given over all those years. Please read that paragraph more times until you get the message.

Chronic illness brings forth numerous emotional storms that cannot be fully described in a single book. However, it is crucial for friends, family, school personnel with children in the family, and medical professionals to remain vigilant and understand that the entire family is experiencing the trauma—the spouse, the children, the close friends, everyone. That is why at times, the family or spouse may seem distrustful or critical of care. Their loved one has endured suffering not just for one hour when they were lying in that bed with urine or feces on them, but for years, including the shifts when low staffing made it impossible to provide adequate care. The family becomes exhausted and occasionally needs to retreat for a few hours. It is not that they don't care or don't want to be there every waking moment; there are emotional and physical limits to what any individual can do. Unfortunately, not all medical staff understand or respond to the needs of the caregivers. Sometimes, caregivers have to deal with nonverbal responses and treatment from staff, and they apologize because they understand the limitations. However, the family must advocate for their loved one. It's important for the family to recognize that healthcare facilities are often understaffed and the existing staff members are overworked. This can also impact the quality of care provided to their loved ones. Exhibiting angry or intolerant behavior towards staff members is not helpful to anyone.

Our Christian faith and belief helped Rick and me stay humble during treatment and mistreatment or absence of care during emergencies. God's grace blessed us many times.

*****

("But the fruit of the Spirit is love, joy, peace, long-suffering, gentleness, goodness, faith, meekness, temperance: against such there is no law." Galatians 5:22)

Chapter 11

Another Call At Work

It was a busy Friday morning in the county school health office when the phone rang, and I picked up. It was Rick's oncologist. She first told me that she did not want Rick to know everything she was about to share with me because he was going to require every bit of physical and emotional strength possible for the next steps. Rick and I had always shared everything, so my heart raced, and I had difficulty hearing at that point. She continued to say that the latest labs confirmed that the leukemia was out of remission. He would need to return to the hospital on Monday morning to resume the most aggressive chemotherapy they could administer; she felt that he would go into total renal failure and would require dialysis very soon. She continued that he was worse clinically than he had ever been and may not return home again. His blood counts for immunity were extremely low. However, we should provide family time over the weekend and allow the grandbabies to visit as tolerated, with no rules unless someone has a fever. She told me to make the weekend as normal as possible, allow him space to do whatever he wished, and she would admit him and begin treatment Monday morning. She called to tell him to enjoy visits with family over the weekend and notified him when his admission to the hospital would be.

Rick had a sense that things were deteriorating rapidly. He had to hold up his jeans with one hand, yet he continued to tend to his garden, a place where he found solace and communicated with God while he worked. His weight loss was alarming, happening at an alarming pace. He made very little eye contact with me, unlike when he was first diagnosed. At that time, they were administering platelet infusions to prevent the severe nosebleeds he had experienced in the beginning.

Jenny had recently been home for a visit from California with her husband and daughters, Jessica and Jacquie. Her daddy had traveled against physician advice a few years earlier to move her to California; he needed to see where his daughter was moving!

That weekend, Kristen came over to the house with the grandkids. Rick had Lily, who was barely old enough to walk and participate in some yard activities, watering and planting flowers around the flagpole and in the garden boxes in front of the porch. It was an incredibly hot day, one of the first few days of May, 2013. Daniel, who was almost 4 years old, barely remembers his grandpa. Rick went to his outbuilding and retrieved his camping tent. His dream was to take Daniel camping and fishing. With some assistance, he set up the large tent. He took the grandkids inside the tent to play. Later, when it was just Daniel and him inside the tent, I witnessed the tent's window roll up, and a small stream of water trickled out. Rick had always mentioned that the boy needed to experience peeing out of the window of a tent, and he made it happen. That had been the entire purpose of setting up the tent on the lawn that hot May morning, and it was subsequently taken down and stored once Daniel finished playing.

As the day progressed, he grew weaker. He spent time talking with Kris, playing with the kids, and sitting in his swing on the front porch. I was concerned about how the heat might dehydrate him and disrupt his renal balance, the things we had been monitoring for so many years. Little did I know that my worry was in vain.

On Monday, during the first week of May 2013, Rick was admitted to the hospital as planned. Orders were in place, and things began moving immediately. He responded well to the treatment for a week, and I even brought him a Mexican meal. He seemed to be doing great that week, as if our prayers had been answered. However, that's when everything changed. It felt like all of his body systems started to rebel. He experienced bleeding from his stomach and bowel, his renal function declined, and he faced a myriad of miserable complications.

In the following days, I would be called out to the hallway where the oncologist would inform me that Rick's blood had been sent to MD Anderson. She discovered that he had a chemically-induced form of leukemia that did not show traditional markers in the lab work. It had never been in remission, and the only option was to treat the symptoms and observe how things progressed, although the outlook was not favorable. Dialysis had to be initiated, which was incredibly restrictive and made him feel even worse. Each session caused his levels to go haywire, requiring new IVs to be administered to balance them again. He had several visits to the ICU, occasionally returning to the Cancer Floor. Unlike our numerous trips to the emergency room over the past year and a half, where he was exposed to unclean and poorly maintained environments, the Cancer Floor was meticulously clean and safe. The care he received was excellent, and his nurses went above and beyond. The entire staff became like instant family. Housekeeping and dietary staff often checked in to see if he needed anything to make him more comfortable. The days were filled with trauma as he felt incredibly sick, lost his hair, and my brother-in-law, Carmel, came to buzz off the rest of his hair during his cancer treatments.

At this time, I needed to take a leave of absence from work because I could no longer balance work responsibilities- I needed to be with him full-time. I had allowed him to be independent as long as possible; the time had come.

Around the second week of May, Rick fell extremely ill. He was unable to eat anything, and even sucking on a popsicle caused bloody stool to ooze from his body. Weak and debilitated, he couldn't stand, go to the restroom, or even use a bedpan. In his opinion, all dignity had been stripped from his existence. How could such a strong man become so sick so quickly?

During this time, I would go back and forth to check on the house, grab a snack, shower, and take short naps whenever possible. Then I would drive back to Charleston. I took care of Rick's bath, assisted him with his personal needs, and prayed for him. Anxiety, the heat in the room, and the discomfort of the dialysis machines made my heart race. Even the gentlest touch caused him pain. He was barely able to talk, and he lay there with his eyes shut. At a point in time, he told me to fetch a pencil and paper because he needed to talk to me.

I anticipated he wanted to discuss business matters, as he was the one who handled bill payments and kept tabs on all our business affairs. Little did I know that there was an elephant in the room waiting to be acknowledged. I sat on the side of the bed, ready to listen and write down anything he wanted to say. He asked me not to speak, just to listen and record everything so I wouldn't forget. Then he uttered the words that shattered my heart: something was broken, and this time, it couldn't be fixed. With his eyes tightly closed, he began detailing his funeral arrangements—his wishes for speakers, songs, and what he wanted the minister to talk about. Rick loved his garden and believed it was where he conversed with God. He requested songs like "In the Garden" and asked the preacher to draw comparisons between the garden and our walk with God. I sobbed as I jotted down every detail, feeling the weight of his impending loss.

I dared to ask a couple of questions, but he made it clear that nothing was up for discussion. At that moment, it felt as though I was in the midst of a war—a piece of my heart was dying as the man I had prayed for over 16 years slipped away. I had never felt such sickness and emptiness in my life. Afterward, I sought solace at the nursing station, sharing with Rick's nurse what had just transpired. She reassured me, drawing on her nursing expertise and explaining that it was not uncommon for critically ill patients to express their final wishes. I tried to accept her reassurance, but deep down, I was shaken to the core.

Two weeks had passed, and he had been sent back to the ICU. He was undergoing routine dialysis in his room, but it never really helped. I hadn't seen so many IVs hanging in a very long time. As his condition deteriorated further in the ICU, they informed us that any family or friends could visit. The next day, a steady stream of friends arrived to see him. Unfortunately, his oncologist was off duty that weekend. Jenny had flown home from California and relieved Kristen and me for the night, but he started experiencing nosebleeds again. I tried to stabilize my dropping blood sugar, packed some snacks that I force-fed myself, and managed to get a couple of hours of sleep. That night, he made the decision to request hospice care. He had simply suffered for far too long, and nothing seemed to be improving, only worsening. He didn't tell me about his decision, as he didn't want me to beg him otherwise. It would only be a matter of hours before the request was made. In the last few days, we had managed to have a few conversations, although he was too sick to talk most of the time. Visits from anyone exhausted him and were emotionally challenging. He often lay with his eyes closed, and very few words were spoken.

Jenny called to inform me that his nose was bleeding. I rushed to the hospital and found that he had slipped into a coma, experiencing occasional seizures. Despite his unconscious state, I could sense that he was aware of our presence. I insisted that Jenny go home and get some rest while Kristen joined me at the hospital. We took care of him, moistening his mouth and providing comfort. Feeling dizzy and needing to stabilize myself, I stepped out for a while. I knew what was happening, and I had to gather myself before returning. I went to Kris' nearby home briefly to regain my composure and then hurried back to the hospital. Kris remained with him during that time. As I stood by his side, I whispered my final words into his ear and softly sang a hymn. I could see his vitals changing on the machines. Kris stepped out momentarily to call Jenny back, and the moment she was outside the door, he peacefully passed away. I immediately called her back into the room. In that very moment, it struck me that the journey we had traveled together for 20 years, the moment I had dreaded all that time, had become a heartbreaking reality.

At that moment, I laid my head down beside him, clutching his hand, and waited for the doctor to pronounce him. Inexplicably, a profound sense of peace enveloped me, a peace that remains unexplainable even as I type these words, a decade later. I tremble and weep uncontrollably. The man whom I loved with every fiber of my being, the father of my children, my soulmate, had passed away. I was incredibly fortunate to have had the opportunity to say goodbye, a privilege that many are not granted. Rick had crossed over the threshold from death into eternal life. He was now completely healed, meeting our Savior and Lord whom we had faithfully trusted in for so many years. Heaven was rejoicing in his arrival. He had lived 61 years on this earth.

*****

As the words of Philippians 1:21 in the King James Version remind me, *"For to me to live is Christ, and to die is gain."*

Chapter 12

The Journey of Grief- Observations by a Nurse and Wife

There are no words to convey how one should live through their grief; it is a daily learning experience. Some days you will succeed, while others you will feel like you're failing. There is no fixed timeline; it's not a process where you simply improve with time. If you love deeply, you will grieve intensely. God will embrace you in His arms during both the good and bad times. No two individuals will grieve in the same way, and neither is wrong in their journey. At times, you may feel as though those observing your life are judging you, thinking they would handle it differently. They may be correct because each person's personality leads them to cope with grief in unique ways.

There are some things that are helpful in grieving:

1. Seek human contact; there is nothing that helps more. Whether you are serving at your church or having lunch with friends, do not isolate yourself. If you are a friend of the deceased, share and talk with the family if there are things you want them to know that will ease their pain.

2. Do not allow others to place you on a timeline for grieving; such constraints do not exist.

3. Play music, any music; it is energy for your soul

4. Read the Psalms in the Bible; David can teach you so much!

5. Seek counsel if your grief becomes overpowering and controls your life to the point you are having physical or emotional symptoms.

6. Seek emergency care if you ever experience suicidal thoughts; there is someone who cares.

7. Before any of these things, read your Bible, pray daily, and develop a stronger relationship with God; thus, you will have more understanding, peace, and a healthier journey in His care.

*****

("In my distress, I cried unto the Lord, and he heard me." Psalm 120: 1)

Chapter 13

Reflections

Just as Rick would emotionally withdraw from me when he was critically ill, he did the same in his final weeks. It was difficult for him to verbalize his feelings throughout life, but that was not it. There was no longer an elephant in the room. I believe the ill individual is processing the transition they are getting ready to experience. The patient can hear and sense the presence of close friends and family. When a patient is dying, their view on death and dying changes if they are a Christian. Their life will soon be a new beginning, free from illness, sadness, worry or stress. Our human minds cannot comprehend all of what they are experiencing, we only grieve their passing, their absence, and our loneliness without them.

I am so thankful for my Christian faith because it changes my perspective, giving me an illustration of God holding me in his arms as I continue this journey.

I wrote this book with the intention of it being more than a somber reflection on Rick and my life. I wanted it to serve as a testament to our prayers, the healing we experienced at different stages of his journey, and the miraculous moments that extended his life. Additionally, I aimed to offer assistance to those currently facing chronic illness, encouraging them to recognize that their emotions are valid and should be shared with their spouse, rather than trying to shield their loved ones from the overwhelming feelings that consume them. My hope is that this book sparks conversations among family members, enabling them to express important thoughts and emotions that may otherwise remain unspoken or unexpressed.

To the friends of the deceased: If you have cherished memories of the deceased expressing special love for their spouse, it is meaningful to share and discuss those memories with the surviving partner. Especially in the early stages of grief, it can be comforting for the bereaved to hear how their loved one spoke affectionately and cared for them, whether it was in private conversations or at work, or even through shared experiences with another friend. Don't hesitate to share positive thoughts and memories you had with the departed loved one.

Sometimes, the most significant contribution you can make to support the surviving spouse is to lend an ear. It can be challenging, as it requires a skill to be learned, but often, all the individual needs is someone to listen and provide a space for them to share their thoughts and feelings, to debrief, right after the loss of their loved one. At times, silence can be immensely valuable, as the person simply needs the reassurance that you are there for them.

In summary, there are certain aspects that will forever remain unspoken, much like how your relationship was private. Some of the topics you lovingly shared will also fall into this category. I can confidently say that I would never have wanted to undertake this journey without God by my side. Only He could provide solace during the countless lonely hours spent at the hospital throughout the years. Only He could bring comfort to my soul when anxiety and fear engulfed us.

And when the time came, only He could grant peace and a dignified passing.

I hope that something within the pages of this book will deeply resonate with every reader, offering solace and alleviating the emotional burden that comes with this journey. I thank my family, friends, and all of the health professionals who shared our journey so many years.

I will forever thank God for the miracles along the way.

I will always treasure the way Rick summarized our life together in the final words spoken to me:

"We've had a good run and seen some good things; I love you."

*****

("And now these three remain: faith, hope and love. But the greatest of these is love." I Corinthians 13: 13 NIV)

God can strengthen any of us through the various trials of life. By His will, we walk this journey until our final home with Him in heaven. If you are not a Christian, consider reading the following scriptures and pray to Jesus for the forgiveness of your sins. Accept Him into your heart so that you will have the Peace that passeth all understanding for your personal journey in life and death.

Steps To Salvation

• Acknowledge and ask for forgiveness of sin:

Acts 3:19: "Repent ye therefore, and be converted, that your sins may be blotted out when the times of refreshing shall come from the presence of the Lord."

• Believe you can be saved by Jesus:

John 3:16: "For God so loved the world that he gave his only begotten Son, that whosoever believeth in him should not perish, but have everlasting life."

• Confess:

I John 1:9: "If we confess our sins, he is faithful and just to forgive us our sins, and to cleanse us from all unrighteousness."

• Receive:

John 1:12: "But as many as received him, to them gave he the power to become the sons of God, even to them that believe on His name...."

Made in the USA
Monee, IL
26 August 2023

41693484R00056